URBAN HYKOOL
The Zen of the City

By
Robert John Keiber

Haiku Poetry

Published by
The Tuxedo Group
Suite 2514
244 Fifth Avenue
New York, New York 10001
212-252-2065

"The world's most famous Zen poet, the
Tang dynasty's legendary Han Shan,
was a ragged beggar who scratched
poems on the cave walls where he lived
and who worked as a helper in the kitchen
of a Zen monastery."

Sam Hamill
The Poetry of Zen.

Dedicated to my father Jack, who loved
the city and walked from Harlem to
Chinatown on the nights he couldn't sleep,
and to all the beautiful city
dwellers he met along the way.

**He sits like Buddha,
mumbles at those who pass by-
But then he might be.**

rjk

Introduction

We think in pictures, not words. Poetry is most capable of capturing the simpler pictures of a moment, the fleeting essence of a minute or two of life. The great Zen poets Basho, Issa and Ryokan were masters of the simple snapshot. It may have been easier back then to be aware of the minor elements of life without i-pods, Blackberries, texting cell phones and a constant barrage of advertisements distracting us each day. To "be aware" is becoming more and more difficult, particularly in the city.

People are actually so pre-occupied and distracted by their handheld technology in the city, that they are actually getting hit by cars crossing city streets. They are entrapped by technology and satisfy themselves with the instant gratification of fast facts from a cyber-wasteland. They are risking and wasting their lives for neurotic entertainment, believing they "must keep in touch." But what are they keeping in touch with? Certainly it's not the world around them. Today's youth may never have heard the phrase "stop and smell the roses", much less appreciate America's own "Zen" poet Robert Frost. How could they? Mr. Frost may not have a page on Facebook. They might have to go to a non-virtual library or bookstore of "real books" to find him.

This book attempts to make simple observations on visual images that every city offers, and in particular New York City. For instance, the subway is a fascinating classroom of human behavior and the street a high speed montage of life flashing before your eyes. But you must make an effort to be aware and stop and smell the roses or, in this case, the roasted pretzels. As Sam Hamill, one of the editors of THE POETRY OF ZEN points out, "In Zen poetry "sabe" (aloneness) and "sabishisa" (loneliness) are essential to the tradition." Certainly this state of isolation is available in the life of any city dweller. Some may think this state is a bad thing, but Zen poets of the past offer these states of being alone as a beautiful thing. Being alone gave them an opportunity to be aware. However, today's generation is in dread fear of being alone. Being alone might force them to be aware. Unfortunately with today's technology they never have to be alone and thus never aware. Indeed, most people would prefer to be high on the cyber space distractions of distorted context and trivia overload, rather than high on the pure pleasure of observing the chaotic beauty surrounding them on a city street. I would like to suggest to the reader that every now and then they just stop and smell the concrete. On a hot rainy day in mid-July you actually can.

"A sudden glimpse. That sudden glimpse
of awareness that occurs
in everyday life becomes the act of compassion."

Chogyam Trungpa
Zen Master

1
Grand Central Station,
and mad men surge at rush hour,
gorgeous woman strut.

2
 The train ticket booth-
Older folks become older,
young children younger.

3
The policeman knows;
"I do what you don't want to,
so I get the gun."

4
Off the morning train,
we trudge up the station ramp,
sheep to the slaughter.

5
Cowboy hat on train,
city's last desperado-
fearless of all men.

6
Angry subway clerk,
"I make more money than you!"
"How much do I make?"

7
Westchester late train,
with Blackberry companion-
long days to the top.

8
Bellows through the train,
her cell phone displayed proudly,
"I have friends to call."

9
Fat man, sound asleep,
fills the train with his snoring.
Pity his poor wife.

10
Two large men on train,
between them an empty seat.
Saving it for me?

11
Applying make-up,
the train her mobile boudoir.
From plain to pretty.

12
"Times Square please" I shout!
Arabic driver looks lost.
I give directions.

13
Pigeons are eagles,
the skyscrapers tall mountains,
taxies buffaloes.

14
Yellow cabs everywhere.
But in Harlem late at night-
No yellow cabs here.

15
Does at little rain
always wash away big cabs?
Just the ones I need.

16
Women at coffee,
both talking so intensely,
their lives so vital.

17
The back, a goddess.
I run up to see her face.
The back, a goddess.

18
Chinese delivers,
cutting through the jaywalkers,
his bike a scalpel.

19
Pretty Asian girl
with surprisingly full rear-
enters McDonalds.

20
My own big backyard,
Central Park in the summer.-
Don't have to mow it.

21
A Tourist wonders,
"Does the city make them nuts
or do nuts come here?"

22
Walking like a duck,
Lincoln Center fat lady
thinks she's a dancer.

23
Walking his daughter,
her skin tight shorts read "Juicy".
What is he thinking?

24
Tight jeans on Broadway,
with a perfect heart shaped butt.
She knows I'm staring.

25
Two lovers in rain
with only one umbrella
Which one gets wetter?

26
"Give me some of that!"
Construction worker taunts girl-
wife and kids at home.

27
On the mid-town streets,
beautiful women walk by,
just ignoring me.

28
A city Summer.
Exposed cleavages, short-shorts.
I don't mind the heat.

29
In the dark doorways,
junkies of tobacco lurk
for their minute fix.

30
An elevator
soon after a smokers break-
a flying ashtray.

31
A big Cohiba,
the old man puffs with pleasure.
Sweet second hand smoke.

32
A midnight parade
running gutter to basement.
Rats go to market.

33
Parcel driver throws
boxes to back of the truck-
each of them marked "fragile".

34
With his mighty staff
he crosses the busy street-
A brave and blind man.

35
Just to be alone
she walks the crowded city.
She is, she is not.

36
Wall Street rants and raves.
In an old miser's pocket
anger is a hole.

37
Hat full of feathers,
he's cooing like a pigeon.
Birdman delivers.

38
"Where were you last night?"
the stranger asks me passing,
wearing his Blue Tooth.

39
The bold street artist
paints on another man's canvas.
Is it theft or art?

40
In a tuxedo,
there stands the new hot artist,
a big bear on skates.

41
Industry lion.
Tyrant in his own office.
A small mouse at home.

42
An older rich man,
sexy, beautiful young girl.
He is not her dad.

43
Ancient couple sits
in a restaurant window,
lonely together.

44
Bald middle aged man
listens as much younger girl
lectures him on life.

45
Face on the subway,
I am in love at West 4th-
Only to lose her.

46
Bloomingdale's beauty.
I stare, she smiles and walks on.
We had a moment.

47
Powerful, striking,
older, she knows what she wants.
It's not me or you.

48
The city was noisy,
they moved to the country.
Brooklyn, home sweet home.

49
A tiny white fence
around tiny Queen's green lawn.
What does it keep out?

50
Headless umbrellas
all marching through the Spring rain.
All black. All five bucks.

51
Mornings in this town
we drink our coffee standing.
Have to keep moving.

52
Ego loves a drunk,
as he holds court at the bar-
Who else knows it all?

53
Girl in her mink coat
chases behind her poodle -
with a plastic cup.

54
Blond in mini skirt
walks her white Great Dane proudly.
No man can compete.

55
Walking two Pit Bulls,
what once hung between his legs,
now tugs on leashes.

56
Ragged woman cries;
"Please don't spit on the sidewalk,
I sleep here, damn it!"

57
He sits like Buddha,
mumbles at those who pass by.
But then he might be.

58
A pile of blankets,
a pile of humanity rests
on a cardboard bed.

59
Dejected, ignored,
he rules on his milk crate throne,
the street, his kingdom.

60
Dirty and angry,
he insults my dear mother-
my feelings unhurt.

61
Stopping all traffic,
she moves her bags full of junk-
for a change of view.

62
Under the overpass
He puts up his plywood wall-
"Good walls, good neighbors."

63
On a cold hard bench
she sits sad, old and lonely,
feeding pet gray squirrels.

64
"You want change?" he shouts.
"Obama for President!"
"Spare a little change?"

65
The lifeless chicken
hangs in the Chinese window.
He has become art.

66
Little Italy,
it gets smaller and smaller,
soon to disappear.

67
He still stands smiling
among a million sorrows.
Does he know something?

68
Old believers pray
in the dark ancient temple,
"St. Patrick, save me."

69
Wale of a siren,
like an early prayer bell
awakens my lost soul.

70
Mother pigeon sits
under air conditioner
making more pigeons.

71
Seems so out of place.
Tuxedo with cello rides
subway to the Met.

72
He swears at the sky.
Even though I can't see them-
maybe they are there

73
Meat Packing District,
skin tight spandex jogging by
packing firm trim meat.

74
Street conversations
only have room for one saint.
You must pick a side.

75
I'll be more careful.
Dead dad came back as a goose,
sucked in by a jet,

76
Breathing city air,
being at the meat of it-
neurotic comfort.

77
Social disorder,
metaphysical disorder,
"May I take your order?"

78
They can't get sunburned
living here in the city-
They just get burned out.

79
Cabs, cabs everywhere.
But when I'm in a hurry-
all "Off Duty" cabs.

80
A tall great city
across from Staten Island,
divides water and sky.

81
Sea of a city
that some people only drink
one shot at a time.

82
"It depends," she cried.
"It depends on what?" He asked.
"I don't know." she sighed.

83
Little control here
over others ignorance.
First control your own.

84
Central Park is a
Garden of Eden by day.
By night devils crawl.

85
He stood on Prince Street,
house phone wired to a purse,
loudly making deals.

86
"You're a drunken fool,
but you remind me of me.
I like you so far."

87
His telescope peeps,
looking from his high rise box
to her high rise box.

88
On a winter stroll
up Central Park West I ask,
"Should a dog wear fox?"

89
The handsome fireman,
Irish eyes, strong Roman nose,
waits as his pop did.

90
Beware your shower.
When a close neighbor flushes,
you will get scalded.

91
Snow slows the city.
Now and then it needs a rest.
Now and then we do.

92
The city in snow,
it always makes everyone
a bit friendlier.

93
Watching from my box,
true, I will never know you,
but still I long to.

94
Welcome to my box.
Is it bigger than your box?
How much was your box?

95
Box on top of box.
Tall glass stacks of big boxes-
Big town of boxes.

96
Walking down the street,
he imagines them all nude -
Lunch time fantasies

97
Impossible here,
to be really alone here.
Yet so many are.

98
Politician swears,
"Safety, progress, the good life!"
Why vote for mad men?

99
Grabbing the paper.
I put money on the stack,
 while the Moslem prays.

100
Cutting through traffic,
slicing between buses, cabs-
bike guy saves money.

101
It rumbles and roars.
Express trains surge through the veins
of its concrete heart.

102
The frustrated poets
sprawl rage across the pages
of the subway tiles.

103
Unemployed, he looks
through binoculars daily,
at working people.

104
The Fifth Avenue bus,
"I'm sorry, no, you first, Please."
 Civilization.

105
He drives a cab, but
thinks he is a musician,
playing his car horn.

106
Sign: "Hungry, homeless,
I need eight hundred thousand
for a nice condo".

107
He barked at people,
"Give some change or be an ass!"
So many asses.

108
"All men are equal,"
they shout from their penthouses-
but never walk here.

109
Washington Square Park,
a hot Sunday afternoon-
Wow, Sixties flashbacks.

110
It must be good art.
A shark in formaldehyde.
You sure can't eat it.

111
Desperate unknowns
standing behind velvet ropes-
to see nobodies.

112
Chelsea galleries,
pile of glass, a tank of dung.
"Art" is everywhere.

113
I will not hurt him.
My mouse boldly strolls my floor.
He knows I'm lonely.

114
Cat greets me at door.
Not because she loves me so.
She is just hungry.

115
On my block I see
eight million stranger's windows
I will never know.

116
Black town cars line up
Masters of the Universe!
Not my Universe.

117
Prophets walk the streets,
"Where's the justice, love, kindness?"
What was the question?

118
We flood the subway,
with hope that, at each days end,
we have dignity.

119
Both freedom and chains.
The old become prisoners,
but the young run free.

120
It holds the world's wealth.
But where do they keep it all?
Why so many poor?

121
Young, brave, expectant,
the dancer hops off the bus,
Babylon, last stop.

122
Towers fell in smoke,
"Oh Babylon has fallen!"
Wrong again, haters.

123
A face on the bus.
In love again for four stops.
At Fifth abandoned.

124
Nice watch on Canal.
Still, I don't have the money
for the time of day.

125
Eight million bodies
walk this city's crowded streets,
each its own city.

126
"I met Jesus here,"
the drunken man says proudly.
"He drinks Budweiser."

127
"Right here," the drunk says.
"I met Jesus, and Bloomberg."
"Who did you vote for?"

128
Each month's first Thursday,
crowding Chelsea galleries-
a strip mall for art.

129
If you teach my child
I will pay you nothing, but-
for a homerun, gold.

130
He rides a limo,
with a beauty, young and hot-
the boy with the bat.

131
The point guard stands tall,
as adoring grown men reach
just to touch his bling.

132
New York Library.
Everything I do not know
quietly lives there.

133
Great lions look on
while he eats his lunch each day,
and the hungry pass.

134
"Jeter is God, right?"
"Only God is God," I say.
"But Jeter is good!"

135
I stroll through the Met,
an oasis of beauty
for the overwhelmed.

136
The nice bartender,
but is he really your friend?
If you tip freely.

137
At the local shrine,
worship at the oak altar,
one drink at a time.

138
"Ten Dream for Life please,
and five Mega, five Lotto."
The poor people's tax.

139
The "Great Melting Pot,"
Now many small villages-
Now the "Great Salad."

140
Never be alone
on New Year's Eve when millions
beckon from Times Square.

141
Strutting down Lennox,
a young man losing his pants.
 shows "Rappers Butt Crack".

142
Into the cross walk
ignoring horns, they protest
the "Don't Walk" signal.

143
Like a star half back
I look for daylight and sprint-
as cars block the box.

144
In the city bank
all customers try their best
to look so honest.

145
Old man on the bench
once gave away his money-
now just his wisdom.

146
In the coffee shop
she doesn't look so lonely
reading a good book.

147
Daylight to midnight,
from big crowds to lone riders,
the subway lives loud!

148
Through narrow neat streets
I pass West Village walk ups-
dead writers call out.

149
From the 99th floor,
they jumped and flew to Heaven.
Showers of angels.

150
Waiting for a bus
I dream of the clear steam in
the cigarette ad.

151
Canyons of mid-town
don't let bright sun or cool breezes.
Find me in shadows.

152
She seemed much bigger.
Ms. Liberty got smaller
as I grew older.

153
Hard to tell some days.
Does God still live in this town,
or did he move West?

154
Not knowing, we flow-
Babylonian chaos
inside Penn Station.

155
Crime does not pay, right?
What is the alternative?
Does poverty pay?

156
Damn, why would she wait
until the front of the line-
to read the menu?

157
Black and rusty bird
on my fire escape so lost-
looking for a tree.

158
Ugly? Beautiful?
Maybe it would be neither-
without being both.

159
At the workday's end
it empties like a bellows-
less full, not empty.

160
It's always buzzing.
Then falls a blessed silence
just before the dawn.

161
While in the health club,
wise elders speak their wisdom
with knowing silence.

162
Rules of street crossing;
Never make reference to
the traffic signal.

163
The same cross-town bus,
and the third sighting of her.
I know she wants me.

164
An afternoon nap,
stretch, shower and hit the street
just looking for love.

165
He comes to work late,
a Monday morning backache-
bad Karma Sutra.

166
A hole in the ground-
so many heroes fell in-
so many still here.

167
There stands proud Brooklyn.
Never was New York City-
but always Brooklyn.

168
Once it was quiet.
Queens was all big sprawling farms.
Now it grows people.

169
On the South Bronx streets,
accustomed to the gunshots-
we pray for our own.

170
A bitchy mistress,
this town makes you so angry-
still can't give her up.

171
"You know who I am?"
"I remember who you were-
You were nicer then."

172
Like a gourmet meal,
exotic city women
come from spicy blends.

173
Down to the front seats,
lights down at Met Matinee-
the savage hordes charge.

.
174
Says she's a model.
She looks like model I guess-
Doesn't everyone here?

175
The moon is so big -
Let's leap from the Brooklyn Bridge
on to its fat face.

176
All the old vampires
cruise the Village on weekends.
There's fresh blood everywhere.

177
A lone sneaker hangs.
Where is the other sneaker?
Where is the guy's foot?

178
You see the sunlight
but you never see the sun-
It's just not allowed.

179
Never knew its hills
until I rode the city -
in a Pedi-cab.

180
So much noise today,
so many silent people.
What makes all the noise?

181
The cool summer breeze
down West Houston to Hudson-
became winter's bite.

182
Bartender poet
reads me all his new poems-
He makes a good drink.

183
Actress from Ohio-
Fresh knife scar crosses her face.
A thief stole her dream.

184
Music everywhere,
Drums, saxophones, and guitars-
Subway sonata.

185
"Can't help you!" he barks.
She wanders off dejected.
He feels sad briefly.

186
Each day they promised-
"Going Out of Business!"
For years they just lied.

187
"I hate you!" she screams,
then throws her wine in his face.
Still, they will soon wed.

188
Dinner, two couples.
Three very busy chatting.
The fourth is cheating.

189
At the East River.
they wait patiently with poles.
But waiting for what?

190
"I love you, hate you!"
"I love this city, hate it,"
 Am I conflicted?

191
Twice a week I pay
to have her listen to me.
Lovers are cheaper.

192
He listens so well.
If I stop being crazy-
he'll lose interest.

193
My building swayed,
as the hurricane pounded.
Man against nature.

194
Difference between
a therapist and a priest?
A sliding window.

195
Please do not come here
to seek peace, sky or mountain-
You will not find them.

196
"She's dazzling, darling."
This big city's new "It" girl.
Soon just another "Was."

197
See bright new Times Square,
where Mickey and Pluto hang.
The new Orlando!

198
Brown, black, white, yellow
human flag of the city
waving through the streets.

199
From my building roof
shine a million temple lights.
I moon sit till dawn.

200
Leaving the alley,
going nowhere for nothing,
he begins each day.

201
At a soup kitchen
she spots her old therapist -
waiting on the line.

202
What's more depressing
than a dark Hell's Kitchen bar-
on a rainy day?

203
To the highest floor,
the Empire State elevator
stops at Heaven's door.

204
Everyone is here.
When you are walking Broadway-
you walk the whole world.

205
Where ever you're from,
if you needed to come here,
you do belong here.

206
I put my change in,
but the Zombie Bus Driver
never looks at me.

207
Run around the streets,
or stop, stand still and let the
streets run around you.

208
In my cute snow globe
all the small white city streets
never turn to slush.

209
It's a mystery-
Meat on a street vendors grill.
How hungry am I?

210
Nibbles his crackers,
shares his small studio freely.
How he loves that mouse.

211
To my small one room!
To my small cat and my mouse!
To my big ex-house!

212
On the city streets
tourist, young girls and mad men-
walking in flip flops.

213
Pizza shops everywhere.
How to find the famous one?
How to find "the" Ray's.

214
Singing like a fool,
his earphones make him tone deaf.
I'm not so lucky.

215
Pregnant girl on bus.
Seated young man ignores her- .
Elder gives up seat.

216
Pretty butterfly
floats down a Chinatown street.
I could not catch her.

217
On a fire hydrant,
puffing on her cigarette-
a vice-president?

218
West Side family
on a Sunday morning stroll
makes me smile with hope.

219
Voluptuous shapes
of Europe's sultry daughters
well stuffed in tight jeans.

220
Children scream with joy.
floating over the new snow-
Prospect Park's winter.

221
Quietly she sits
Zazen in Strawberry Fields
waiting for her John.

222
Claimed he could not see
America from Times Square.
Where was he looking?

223
In her apartment
she leaves the radio on low,
pretending he's there.

224
Easy to forget.
We cut across the earth's core
when we cross mid-town.

225
There is no such thing!
Against the laws of nature!
A quiet Irish bar.

226
Hands me a flyer,
so I take it, I thank her-
then throw it away.

227
Two lone figures sit
on a Gramercy Park bench
like crows on a branch.

228
A city snow storm,
and my window seat is bliss.
I've nowhere to be.

229
Old man's last request-
"bury me near the Park Zoo
to hear children laugh."

230
NYU students
shop the upper Eastside streets
on bulk garbage night.

231
Dreams of her island,
the taste of sweet, fresh mangos,
here five dollars each.

232
An empty Wall Street,
almost nothing is moving-
still its power throbs.

233
To love the city
you must first leave the city,
then return to it.

234
the "People to Watch"
now wait in unemployment,
and so I watch them.

235
A magic kingdom,
where criminals become stars
and stars become cons.

236
With the peep shows gone,
he doesn't go there anymore.
It makes him too sad.

237
Armed soldiers, bomb dogs.
Beirut, Israel, Moscow?
Grand Central Station.

238
Grew old together,
lovers, but never married-
Two fine gentlemen.

239
An education,
early morning subway ride-
Real Life 101.

240
All about numbers.
You pursue them. You get them.
You never call them.

241
One time the tallest,
then it wasn't. Then it was-
Empire State Building.

242
To make a friend here,
you embrace everybody's neurosis,
then their sanity.

243
A good city friend
never minds your business,
while watching your back.

244
Let it just happen.
Don't try to control this town.
Nobody can own it.

245
Closed some schools in Queens,
firehouses in East Harlem.
Built a new ball park!

246
In tight mini shorts.
a striking seductive pose-
but she is a he.

247
Three fat dogs and I
toast with the ale of Chumleys.
"To all dead writers!"

248
Here only two speeds-
never stop, never neutral,
just fast and faster.

249
Many analysts,
so many crazy people-
They keep them crazy.

250
To a shrink in fur,
"Did you kill that animal?"
"Died of depression."

251
Each cab, deli, bar
a school of philosophy
in search of meaning,

252
Like never before,
the busy streets of Harlem-
filled with suits and ties.

253
God, what would happen
if the sirens went silent?
How would we all sleep?

254
No movie stars here.
Just some neighborhood fellas,
who make some movies.

255
It doesn't have time.
for strategy or logic.
It needs things that work.

256
Independent souls,
all just doing their own thing-
Orderly chaos.

257
Dark chocolate skin,
behold the African Queen-
her elegant proud strut!

258
Her full butt swings free
walking in high heel sandals-
to a Salsa beat.

259
Full beards, tall black hats,
white shirts and long black wool coats-
on an August day.

260
Bad experience,
but strong determination
not to give it up.

261
The mighty Hudson
at the end of Morton Street-
a Jersey sunset.

262
Pigeons do not care.
Each fire escape, each statue,
their private bathroom.

263
Never too noisy
to always hear "God bless you"
after a big sneeze.

264
A moving ink brush
paints on snowy Central Park-
a black dog running.

265
A Harlem window,
street traffic her only friends-
an old woman sits.

266
Between the sirens
and the roar of the El tracks,
a new baby cried.

267
You cannot drain it.
Like an old seasoned teacher-
it never empties.

268
You can't compare it.
Like a fantastic orgasm,
there is just no time.

269
I'm never bored
with a big city so filled
with strange distractions.

270
One with dignity,
Another on just pure ego-
Both will get you through,

271
Sad to be alone
on yet another New Year's Eve.
How Time Square beckons.

272
Pale legs, mini-skirt,
jet black hair, red cowboy boots-
Korean cowgirl.

273
Rain pounds my window,
I watch the lightning in awe-
Electric city.

274
The big city grows
with McDonalds, Burger King.
The people grow too.

275
Her dog has cancer.
His daughter, a brain tumor-
She and butcher hug.

276
A cheerleader face,
but the tattoo on her back,
an elephant head?

277
Friend, there is no point
waiting for the Hummingbird.
There's no place to land.

**But if my friend, from time to
time, you hear the sounds of
ghostly laughter, it's all the
great mad poets, dead,
just dropping in to listen.**

**Kuan Hsiu
832-912**